mind workout puzzles

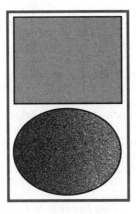

TERRY H. STICKLES
Illustrated by James Michaels

Sterling Publishing Co., Inc.
New York

Edited by Jeanette Green
Copyedited by Liz Kaufman

3   5   7   9   10   8   6   4   2

Published by Sterling Publishing Company, Inc.
387 Park Avenue South, New York, N.Y. 10016
Previously published under the title
Mindstretching Puzzles © 1994 by Terry H. Stickels
Distributed in Canada by Sterling Publishing
c/o Canadian Manda Group, One Atlantic Avenue, Suite 105
Toronto, Ontario, Canada M6K 3E7
Distributed in Great Britain and Europe by Cassell PLC
Wellington House, 125 Strand, London WC2R 0BB, England
Distributed in Australia by Capricorn Link (Australia) Pty. Ltd.
P.O. Box 704, Windsor, NSW 2756 Australia

Sterling ISBN 0-8069-9658-7

Contents

Acknowledgments

I'd like to thank the following people for their helpful suggestions in putting this book together: Frank Bernhart, Dr. Jamie Campbell (Rochester Institute of Technology), Martin Gardner, Dr. John Harper (Chairman of Mathematics Department, University of Rochester), Michael Michalko, Doug Oathout, Linda Quinlan, Dr. Abbie Salny, Phyllis Stewart, Dr. David Suits (Rochester Institute of Technology), Susan Wojciechowski, John Wolfe, and my editor, Jeanette Green.

Special thanks to Judy Skillington, Liz Kaufman, and my wife, Kelsey Flower, for their tireless efforts and encouragement.

Introduction

Most of us enjoy the challenge and fun a good mental puzzle offers. Of course, we all have different preferences. Some people only work crosswords. Some like brain teasers involving logic or mathematics, including analogy and series puzzles. Others favor puzzles with pictures that involve the way we perceive objects or space.

The abilities we exercise while working puzzles can also be applied in school, business, and everyday life. Most experts in the thinking business believe these skills can be sharpened with practice.

If you believe that mental challenges and fun are mutually exclusive, think again. Becoming a better problem solver isn't much different from working to become a better athlete. The initial growth pangs can be frustrating, but with patience and practice, skills can be developed; and you will find that the puzzles become more fun.

The puzzles in this book were constructed to provide fun, and to increase mental flexibility, allowing you to explore different approaches. This little workout may aid you in other puzzles or problems you encounter in everyday life.

If you are conversant with first-year algebra, you may find it useful for a few puzzles. But it's not required. In fact, it isn't necessary to have any specialized training or discipline. This book offers some hints along the way, but basically, you are left to your own devices.

These puzzles are not presented in order of difficulty. And what's easy for you may be difficult for someone else and vice versa. Don't give up right away if you find a particular puzzle difficult! Mentally stretch it, bend it, and spin it. Turn it upside down, inside out, and approach it from every avenue you can, even if that seems absurd. You may be surprised at how quickly you gain mental agility.

I trust that you'll find these mental gymnastics rewarding, and that they will encourage you to look at problems from different perspectives. More than anything, have a good time!

You'll find solutions are in the Answers section at the back of the book. These are the answers we've found, but maybe you'll come up with more!

QUESTIONS

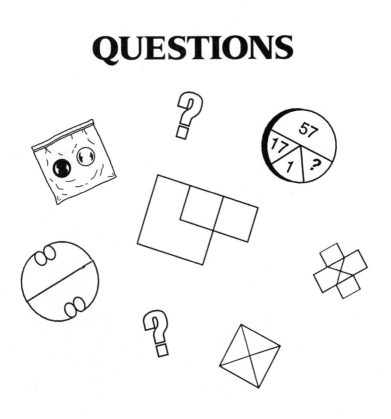

For the uninitiated, the first three puzzles are called cryptarithms or, more precisely, alphametics. Puzzle creator J. A. H. Hunter coined the term *alphametic* to designate words that have meaning, rather than the random use of letters found in cryptarithms.

The object of this type of puzzle is to replace letters with digits. Each letter must represent the same digit, and no beginning letter of a word can be zero. If properly constructed, alphametics can be deduced logically.

In the first puzzle, my verbal arithmetic leaves something to be desired. Assign a number to each letter to correct my addition. Hint: Make a box or chart to consider the possibilities of different values.

1.
```
    ONE
    ONE
    ONE
    ONE
    ───
    TEN
```

2.
```
    NOON
    MOON
    SOON
    ────
    JUNE
```

3. This third alphametic is more difficult than the first two, and there is more than one correct answer. Hint: create more than one chart of values.

THIS
IS
NOT
WITH
WHICH

4. If A = 2 and B + P + F = 24, what are the values of Q and S? Hint: Consider whole numbers only.

A + B = Z
Z + P = T
T + A = F
F + S = Q
Q − T = 7

5. Here is a cube presented from four different perspectives. One of the views is incorrect. Can you tell which one?

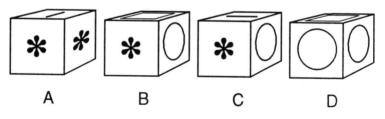

A   B   C   D

Flattened Cube

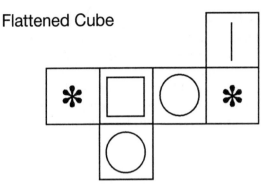

6. Puzzle 5 shows one way you can unfold a cube into two dimensions. Here are two other ways to unfold a cube.

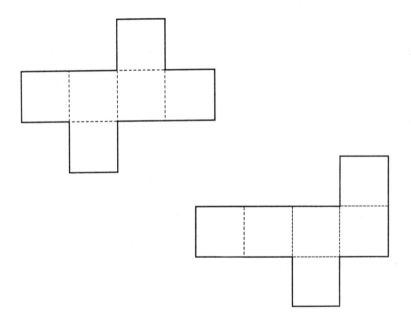

How many additional ways can you find to illustrate a cube in two dimensions?

7. Your boss has asked you to purchase three different types of ballpoint pen. The first costs 50¢, the second $5.50, and the third $9.50. He has given you $100 and told you to purchase 100 pens in any combination as long as you spend exactly $100 for 100 pens. Just one solution is possible. Can you find it? Hint: Familiarity with solving simultaneous equations would be helpful here.

8. Three of these five figures fit together to create a triangle. Which ones are they?

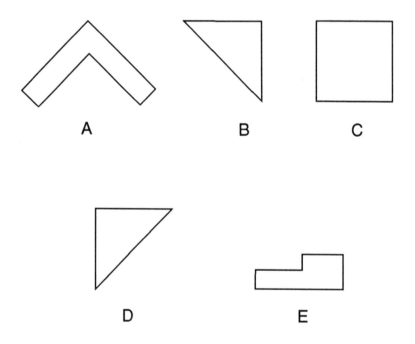

A   B   C

D   E

9. Here's a problem that will test your "layered thinking" ability. Give yourself about a minute to solve this puzzle.

Imagine that you have four kings and three queens from an ordinary deck of playing cards. (If you have access to a deck, the puzzle is more fun.)

The object of the game is to arrange the seven cards in an order that will result in an alternating pattern of K, Q, K, Q, K, Q, K. The seven cards must be held facedown. Move every other card, beginning with the first, to the bottom of the deck. Beginning with the second card, place every other card faceup on the table to reach the desired alternating pattern.

Remember, the first card goes to the bottom of the facedown pile, the second card goes faceup on the table, the third card goes to the bottom, the fourth card goes faceup, etc., until all seven are on the table.

What is the beginning arrangement of the cards?

10. Mary has placed two chocolate cupcakes in one drawer of her kitchen. In another drawer, she has placed a chocolate and a vanilla cupcake; and in a third drawer, two vanilla cupcakes. Her brother knows the arrangement of the cupcakes, but doesn't know which drawers contain each arrangement.

Mary opens one of the drawers, pulls out a chocolate cupcake, and says to her brother, "If you can tell me what the chances are that the other cupcake in this drawer is chocolate, I'll let you have any cupcake you like."

What are the chances that the other cupcake is chocolate?

11. A team of cryptologists is in the process of developing a four-digit code that can never be broken. They know that if the code begins with 0, 5, or 7, it can be cracked. What is the greatest number of four-digit codes the team can use that won't be broken?

12. Assuming that P, Q, and R have values other than those already used, what number, excluding 0, is it impossible for R to be?

$$
\begin{array}{r}
2\ P\ 4 \\
Q\ 5 \\
+\ R\ 7 \\
\hline
4\ 0\ 6
\end{array}
$$

13. If 7^{33} is divided by 10, what will the remainder be? You may get the wrong answer if you try to solve this on some calculators.

14. While reading a certain newspaper, you notice that four pages of one section are missing. One of the missing pages is 13. The back page of this section is 40. What are the other three missing pages?

15. If the first three of the following statements are true, is the conclusion true or false?

All Nebraskans are Cornhusker fans.

Some Cornhusker fans are also Hawkeye fans.

Some Hawkeye fans are also Cyclone fans.

Therefore, some Nebraskans are Cyclone fans.

16. In a strange, distant land, they have a slightly different number system than ours. For instance, $4 \times 6 = 30$ and $4 \times 7 = 34$. Based on this, what is the value of $5 \times 4 \times 7$ in this land? Hint: Remember this is a number *system*.

17. Ann, Boobie, Cathy, and Dave are at their monthly business meeting. Their occupations are author, biologist, chemist, and doctor, but not necessarily in that order. Dave just told the biologist that Cathy was on her way with doughnuts. Ann is sitting across from the doctor and next to the chemist. The doctor was thinking that Boobie was a goofy name for parents to choose, but didn't say anything.

What is each person's occupation?

18. The French Open Tennis Tournament has seven rounds of single elimination of its men's singles competition. This includes the championship match, and there are no byes.

How many men's singles players originally enter when play begins?

19. See if you can establish a pattern to fill in the fourth grid in this sequence puzzle.

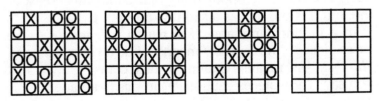

20. The sum of the infinite series ½ + ¼ + ⅛ + ¹⁄₁₆ ... equals 1.

What is the sum of the infinite series ¼ + ¹⁄₁₆ + ¹⁄₆₄ + ¹⁄₂₅₆ ... ?

21. This puzzle requires analytical reasoning. Determine the relationships between the figures and words to find two solutions.

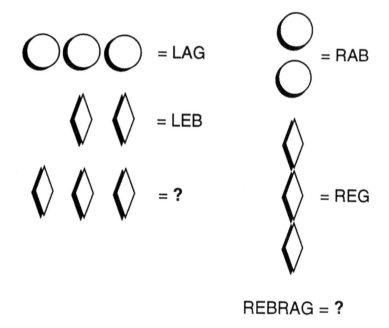

REBRAG = ?

22. Here's another opportunity to use analytical reasoning, but this puzzle has a slightly different twist.

In a foreign language, "*Kaf navcki roi*" means "Take three pieces"; "*Kir roi palt*" means "Hide three coins"; and "*Inoti kaf kir*" means "Cautiously take coins." How would you say "Hide pieces cautiously" in this language?

23. When the proper weights are assigned, this mobile is perfectly balanced. Can you determine the three missing weights? Hint: Distance$_1$ × weight$_1$ = distance$_2$ × weight$_2$.

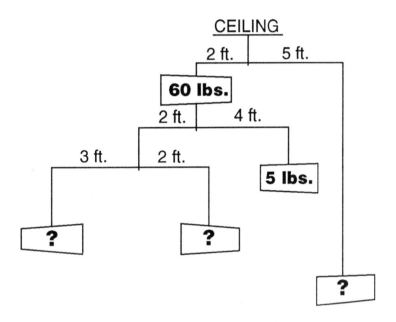

Convert these measurements and weights into metrics, if you wish. (Feet × 0.3 = meters. And pounds × .45 = kilograms.)

24. Seventy-eight percent of all people are gum chewers, and 35 percent of all people are under the age of fifteen. Given that a person has been selected at random, what is the probability that the person is not a gum chewer and above age fifteen?

25. What is the next letter in this series?

A   B   D   O   P   Q   _?_

26.   **A.** 2^{65}

  B. $(2^{64} + 2^{63} + 2^{62} \ldots 2^2 + 2^1 + 2^0)$

In comparing the values of A and B, which of these statements is correct?

B is 2^{64} larger than A.

A is 2^{64} larger than B.

A and B are equal.

B is larger than A by 1.

A is larger than B by 1.

27. Classic puzzles are fun to revisit now and then, especially if there's a new twist.

In this puzzle, see if you can be as successful as John in retrieving water for his mother. The new twist? The buckets are different sizes.

John's mother told him to go to the river and bring back exactly 9 gallons of water in one trip. She gave him a six-gallon bucket and a five-gallon bucket to complete his task. Of course, John's mother told him she'd bake his favorite cake if he came back with the 9 gallons.

John had his cake and ate it, too. Can you?

28. In the world of physics, sometimes things that appear to move forward are actually moving backward. Knowing this, can you complete this analogy?

EMIT : STAR :: TIME : ____?____

29. What is the next number in this series?

1   9   18   25   27   21   ____?____

30. Nine men and seven women pick as much corn in five days as seven men and eleven women pick in four days. Who are the better corn pickers and by how much?

31.   1881 : 1961 :: 6009 : ____?____

Puzzles 32 to 38 are all composed of numbers, but that doesn't necessarily mean that the numbers contained in any given problem are mathematically related. Your mind will have to be flexible to determine what type of relationship the numbers in the series have with each other. There are no holds barred, and each puzzle may have a solution more obvious than you realize at first.

32. What is the next number in this series?

1   2   4   13   31   112   __?__

33. What is the next number in this series?

1   4   2   8   5   7   __?__

Hint: This might be just a fraction of what you think.

34. What is the missing number in this series?

9   3   15   7   12   __?__   13   5   17   11

35. What is the next number in this series?

0   2   4   6   8   12   12   20   16   __?__

36. What is the missing number in this series?

16   21   26   26   12   __?__   19

37. What is the next number in this series?

$$3 \quad 4 \quad 11 \quad 16 \quad 27 \quad 36 \quad \underline{\quad ? \quad}$$

38. What is the next number in this series?

$$224 \quad 1 \quad 8 \quad 30 \quad 5 \quad \underline{\quad ? \quad}$$

❁ ❁ ❁ ❁

39. No puzzle book would be complete without at least one anagram. Here is a phrase that, when unscrambled, spells the name of a famous person. The phrase gives a small hint relating to the person's identity.

BEEN IN STAR LITE

40. Imagine a 3 × 3 × 3-inch opaque cube divided into twenty-seven 1-inch cubes. Quickly, what are the maximum number of 1-inch cubes that can be seen by one person from any point in space?

41. What are the values of §, ⊗, and ¶?

$$\S + \S + \S + \otimes = \S + \S + \otimes + \otimes + \otimes = \P + \P$$

$$\P - \S = 6$$

42. Bill is standing on the ground, looking directly at one of the faces of a new museum built in the shape of a four-sided pyramid. All the sides are identical.

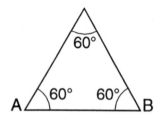

At night, each edge of the pyramid is illuminated with an array of colored lights. Bill's friend Judy is in an airplane touring the area. When her plane, which is several thousand feet high, flies directly over the top of the pyramid, Bill asks her, via walkie-talkie, if she can tell what angle lines A and B make at the peak of the pyramid. Judy answers without hesitation, but it's not what Bill expected. Why?

43. Below are four grids. See if you can determine the logic used in arriving at each successive grid. What would the next grid look like?

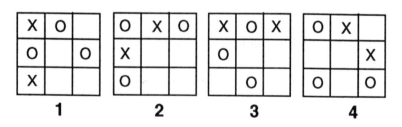

44. Of the four choices below, which best completes this figure analogy?

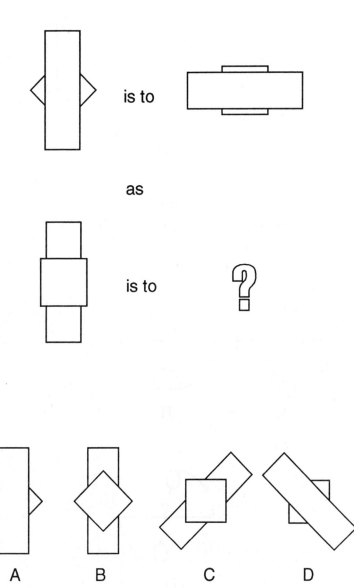

45. Of the four choices below, which best completes this figure analogy?

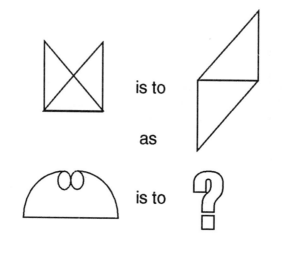

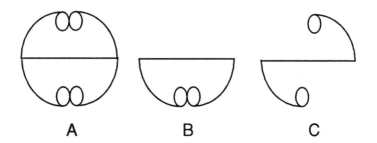

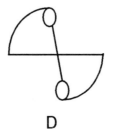

46. Which of the five choices completes this analogy?

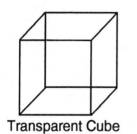 is to

Transparent Cube

Transparent
Tetrahedron

as

 is to

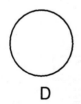

A

B

C

D

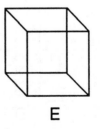

E

47. Complete this analogy.

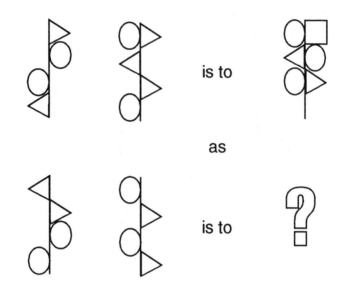

48. Which one of the following figures does not belong? Hint: Don't consider symmetry.

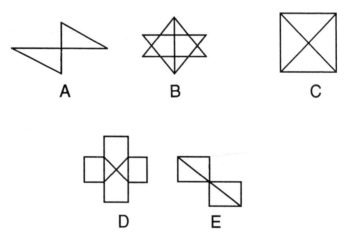

49. A northbound freight train with 100 boxcars will soon meet a southbound freight train with 100 boxcars in single-track territory. They'll meet near a siding track that has a maximum capacity of 80 boxcars. The engines of the southbound train are too heavy to enter any portion of the siding trackage.

With the following information, it is possible for the two trains to get around each other and continue on their trip in the same direction as they started? If so, how?

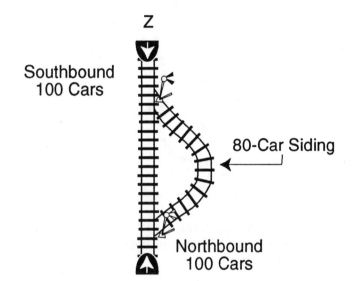

Basic RR Rules

No cars may roll freely by themselves.

All cars and engines have couplers on both ends.

The siding track has switches on both ends.

Engines can move in either direction.

Both train have radio communications and cabooses.

50. An old puzzle asks how many revolutions a rotating coin can make around a duplicate fixed coin in one full rotation. The answer is two. This is a variation of that puzzle, and you may be surprised at the answer.

A rotating gear in a diesel engine revolves around two fixed gears and looks like this.

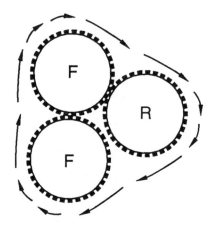

All three gears are identical in size. How many revolutions will Gear R make in one full rotation around the fixed gears?

51. English puzzler Henry Dudeney was a master at creating all types of intriguing train puzzles. From the speeds of roaring locomotives to the times on station clocks, his train puzzles demonstrated elegant simplicity while testing the solver's deductive reasoning power.

In keeping with the spirit of Dudeney's train puzzles, Professor Fractal was taking his best math-prize student to Kensington Station to board a train for Leeds, for the British Isles Math Contest. As they entered the depot, the station clock chimed six o'clock. The professor turned to his math whiz and said, "If you can tell me at what time, immediately prior to six o'clock, the hands of the clock were exactly opposite each other, I'll buy you dinner before your departure."

The student enjoyed a delicious London broil. What was the exact time in hours, minutes, and seconds when the hands of the clock were opposite each other, immediately prior to six o'clock?

52. Nitram Rendrag, the world's most renowned puzzle creator, often rents a private dining car on the Charlotte–Greensboro–Charlotte turn-around shuttle. The railroad charges Rendrag $120 for the trip. On a recent trip, the conductor informed Rendrag that there were two students at the Franklin station who wished to go from Franklin to Greensboro and back to Franklin. Franklin is halfway between Charlotte and Greensboro. Rendrag asked the conductor to let the students ride with him.

When the students boarded Rendrag's car, he said, "If you can tell me the mathematically correct price you should pay for your portion of the trip, I'll let you ride for free. Remember, your answer has to be mathematically equitable for all of us." How much should the students pay for their journey?

53. Sara rows down the Snake River at a rate of 4 m.p.h. with the current. After she's traveled for two hours, she turns around and rows back against the current to where she started. It takes her four hours to return. What is Sara's rowing rate in still water? What is the rate of the Snake River?

54. See if you can deduce the logic of the letters in and around the circles to determine what the missing letter is inside the last circle.

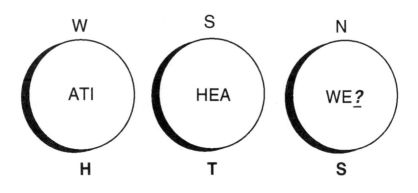

55. What's the missing number?

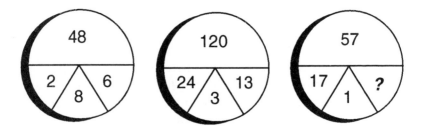

56. Candace is Jane's daughter's aunt's husband's daughter's sister. What is the relationship between Candace and Jane?

57. If one type of weight can balance either 5 gold coins or 4 silver coins, then ten weights of the same type can balance 20 gold coins and how many silver coins in the same scale pan?

58. Sometimes in school or business, we are given information that looks impossible to decipher, only to find out that applying a little "elbow grease" aids in sorting things out. Below are several statements that attempt to form some relationships between the letters A, B, C, and D, and the numbers 1, 2, 3, and 4. Using the following information, see if you can straighten out this confusion and identify each letter with its associated number.

> If A is 1, then B is not 3.
>
> If B is not 1, then D is 4.
>
> If C is 3, then D is not 2.
>
> If C is not 2, then D is 2.
>
> If D is 3, then A is not 4.

Hint: Make a grid with A, B, C, and D on one side and 1, 2, 3, and 4 on the other. Then make some assumptions.

59. Linda wants to drain the water out of a 55-gallon barrel. She has the choice of using either a 2-inch-diameter hose or two 1-inch-diameter hoses to drain the barrel. Which will drain the barrel faster—the 2-inch hose or the two 1-inch hoses? Will they drain the water equally fast?

60. In this alphametic, if you find that one of the letters is equal to nine, then another letter must equal 5 and still another must be 4.

$$
\begin{array}{rl}
A & \text{FIVE} \\
+\ A & \text{FOUR} \\
\hline
\text{IF} & \text{NINE}
\end{array}
$$

61. It seems that every puzzle writer has a friend who is a brilliant logician and who makes a living solving impossible problems for the government or tracking down criminals.

Molly O'Coley is of that rare breed. The 'Mazin' Ms. Molly, as she's known to Scotland Yard, sent me a note some time ago about a notorious international criminal who was jailed due to her efforts. Much secrecy had surrounded the trial because the prosecution didn't want the public to know the large sum of money recovered by Ms. Molly. They felt that information might hinder future efforts to bring the criminal's associates to trial.

Below is the total contents of Ms. Molly's note to me. Each letter of this note stands for a number, and the total is the sum that Ms. Molly recovered. Can you find the exact amount?

32

$$
\begin{array}{r}
\text{T R A I L} \\
+\ \text{T R I A L} \\
\hline
\text{G U I L T Y}
\end{array}
$$

$$Y = 3$$

Note: I later discovered that the Y = 3 also indicated the number of associates the criminal had. Ms. Molly found them in Stuttgart and had them extradited to London.

62. After trying several times to reach my wife by phone and failing, due to problems with the telephone, I arrived home to find this curious coded message left next to the telephone. Can you decipher my wife's message?

9 3 6 8   8 6   2 8 9   2   6 3 9   7 4 6 6 3

63. There are 100 students applying for summer jobs in a university's geology/geography department. Ten of the students have never taken a course in geology or geography. Sixty-three of the students have taken at least one geology course. Eighty-one have taken at least one geography course.

What is the probability that of the 100 applicants any student selected at random has taken either geography or geology, but not both?

How many students have taken at least one course in both geology and geography?

64. Here's another old puzzle with a different twist. Two friends were talking, and the first one said, "Do you remember the brainteaser about a drawer full of black and blue socks?" His friend replied he wasn't sure. "The object is to determine the minimum number of socks you'd have to pick in the dark in order to have a pair of the same color," said the first friend. "Yes," said the second friend, "I remember. The answer is three." "That's right," replied the storyteller. "Quickly now, tell me the minimum number of socks you'd need to take from the drawer if it contained twenty-four blue socks and twenty black socks and you wanted to be assured of a pair of black socks?"

65. This puzzle is a variation of the game nim, named by Harvard mathematics professor Charles Bouton in 1901. Mathemagician Martin Gardner discusses a version of the game in his book *Entertaining Mathematical Puzzles.*

In Gardner's version, coins are arranged like this:

Two players take turns removing the coins. More than one coin can be removed on a turn as long as they are in the same row. The person who is forced to take the last coin is the loser. Gardner asks the reader if an ironclad winning first move can be determined. The answer is yes. The first player removes three coins from the bottom row.

In our version of nim, an extra coin is added to the top so that the ten coins are arranged like this.

The rules are basically the same, except that in our game, if more than one coin is removed from any row, the coins must be adjacent to each other. For example, if a coin had been removed from the bottom row by a player, the other player may *not* pick up the remaining three coins.

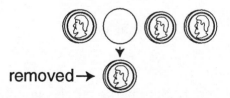

removed →

In this case, the second player may pick up the coin on the left or either or both on the right. In our version, there are two winning first moves. What are they?

66. The numbers 1 through 6 are arranged so that any number resting between and below two other numbers is the difference between those two numbers.

Using numbers 1 through 10, fill in the **X**'s below to create a "difference triangle" with the same conditions. If you'd like a little stiffer challenge, try this using the numbers 1 through 15 in five rows.

67.   (17:8) as (25:7) :: (32:5) as (___?___ : ___?___)

68. Logician George Summers's puzzles are among the best. His logic brainteasers offer a clear, straightforward presentation of the puzzle, yet fully test the deductive reasoning process of even the best puzzle enthusiasts. His book *The Great Book of Mind Teasers & Mind Puzzlers* will keep you busy for days.

In one of his creations, which could be called the "letter cross," letters represent numbers, and you must make several deductions to come up with the value of each letter.

Here is a version of a letter cross puzzle. Although not particularly difficult, it still requires several steps for its solution. Solve this, and you'll be ready to tackle some of Summers's crunchers.

$$A \ B \ C \ D$$
$$E$$
$$F$$
$$G \ H \ I \ J$$

$$A + B + C + D = D + E + F + G = G + H + I + J = 17$$

$A = 4$ and $J = 0$. Using all digits from 0 through 9 only once, find the values for B, C, D, E, F, and G.

There is more than one correct answer. Several numbers are interchangeable.

69. Here's a punchy clue to a series question.

Cubes and squares can be one and the same,
But if this so happens, they need a new name.
Squbes sounds OK, so I'll leave it at that,
But can you now tell me where the next one is at?

64   729   4096   15625   ___?___

70. There are five boxes such that Box C fits into Box A, Box D fits into Box B, Box C is not the smallest, and Box A is not the largest.

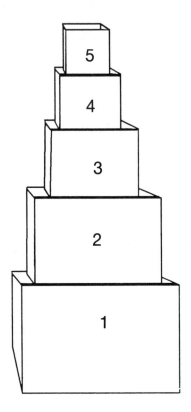

As you can see, Box 1 is the largest and each progressive box is smaller, so that Box 5 is the smallest. The number of the box that represents Box A plus the number of the box that represents Box E is equal to the number of the box that represents Box D plus the number of the box that represents Box C. Determine the size of Boxes A through E from largest to smallest.

71. Three identical bags contain colored balls. Each bag has one red and one white ball. A ball is drawn out of Bag 1, another out of Bag 2, and another out of Bag 3.

What are the chances that you'll end up with exactly 2 white balls?

Bag 1　　　　Bag 2　　　　Bag 3

72. At a gathering of mathematicians, everyone shook hands with four other people, except for two people, who shook hands with only one other person.

If one person shakes hands with another, each person counts as one handshake.

What is the minimum number of people who could have been present? What is the total number of handshakes that took place?

73. You've just thrown your first two dice in a crap game and your point is 10. This means that you must continue to roll the dice until you roll another 10 to make your point. If you roll a 7 before you roll another 10, you lose.

What are your chances of winning with 10 as your point?

74. This game, often called the triangle pegboard game, has been around a long time and offers a good challenge. Maybe you've seen it in restaurants throughout the country.

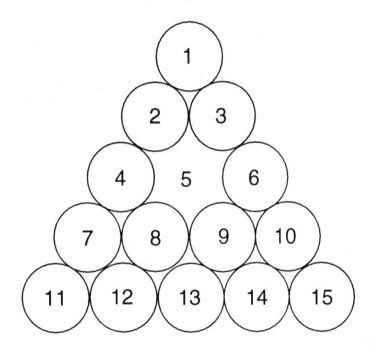

The object of the game, which can also be played with coins, is to jump one peg over another, staying inside the triangle. After jumping over a peg, remove that peg. The goal is to end up with only one peg. Begin with 14 pegs or coins and leave the middle hole open. There is only one solution (two if you count its mirror image). If you've tried this puzzle, you know that it can drive you crazy if you get off on the wrong track.

Below are the first six moves towards the correct solution. Of course, if you want to go it alone, stop reading here.

Take fourteen markers or coins and arrange them as shown. Don't forget to remove a marker after you've jumped over it. Here's your start.

Step 1—Move ⑫ to ⑤.

Step 2—Move ⑩ to ⑧.

Step 3—Move ⑭ to ⑫.

Step 4—Move ③ to ⑩.

Step 5—Move ② to ⑨.

Step 6—Move ⑦ to ②.

There are thirteen jumps in all. The remaining seven moves are in the Answers section.

75. Three straight cuts on a single plane through a cube will result in a maximum of eight pieces. What is the maximum number of pieces that will result when four planar cuts are made through a cube? The slices may not be rearranged between cuts.

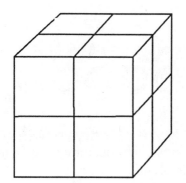

76. Take three coins and arrange them like this.

Now, if you wanted to turn the triangle upside down using the minimum number of moves, you would move Coin 1 below Coins 2 and 3 like this.

What is the minimum number of coins you need to move to turn the following triangle upside down?

Can you find a general pattern or formula for predicting how many coins you must move to turn any triangle of N length upside down?

77. Below are five different sides of a solid object constructed out of several identical cubes fused together. What does the sixth side look like?

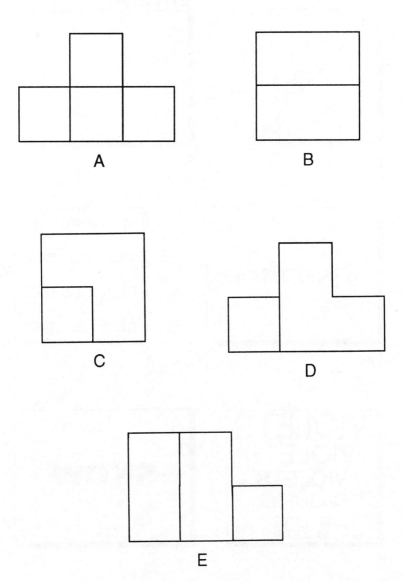

A

B

C

D

E

78. I'm not sure these puzzles have a definitive name. They are not particularly difficult and can be a lot of fun, especially at a party or at family gatherings.

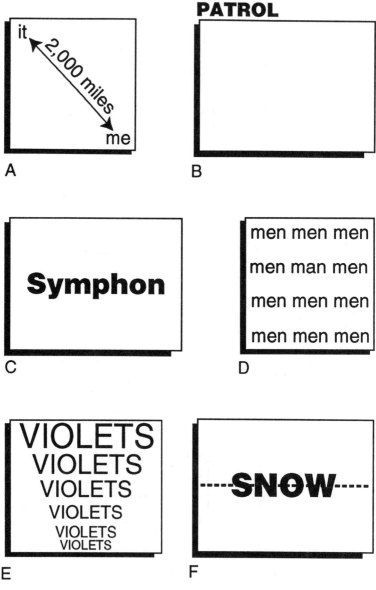

A

B

PATROL

C

Symphon

D

men men men
men man men
men men men
men men men

E

VIOLETS
VIOLETS
VIOLETS
VIOLETS
VIOLETS
VIOLETS

F

----**SNOW**----

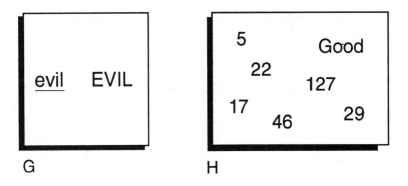

G   H

After you play with these, see if you can come up with some of your own. The object is to guess the words or phrases represented in or around each box. That's all there is to it.

79. Imagine that you must build a tunnel through eight identical cubes. The tunnel must be continuous and start from any of the three exposed faces of Cube 1. The tunnel has to pass through each of the eight cubes only once, and it cannot cut through any place where more than two cubes meet. How many cubes must be excluded as the tunnel's final or exit cube? What are their numbers?

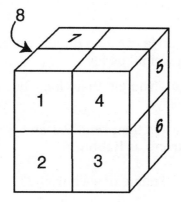

80. Two rockets are launched simultaneously from two different positions.

Rocket A will land at the same spot from which Rocket B was launched, and Rocket B will land at the same spot where Rocket A was launched, allowing a small distance to the left or right to avoid a midair collision.

The rockets are launched from the same angle, and therefore travel the same distance both vertically and horizontally. If the rockets reach their destinations in one and nine hours, respectively, after passing each another, how much faster is one rocket than the other?

81. Four friends, Bob, Bill, Pat, and Tom, are nicknamed Rabbit, Walleye, Fly, and Bear—but not necessarily in that order.

    a. Pat can run faster than Rabbit, but can't lift as much weight as Fly.

    b. Rabbit is stronger than Tom, but slower than Walleye.

    c. Bob is faster than both Pat and Bear, but not as strong as Rabbit.

What is the nickname of each friend?

82. Arrange twelve toothpicks into a sort of window pane. Rearrange only three of them to create eight different triangles of any size. Consider the gap between two connecting toothpicks as a continuous line.

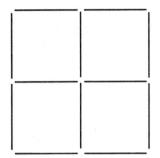

83. A certain blend of grass seed is made by mixing Brand A at $9.00 a pound with Brand B at $4.00 a pound. If the blend is worth $7.00 a pound, how many pounds of Brand A are needed to make 40 pounds of the blend?

84. Here is a sequence of five figures. What would the sixth figure look like?

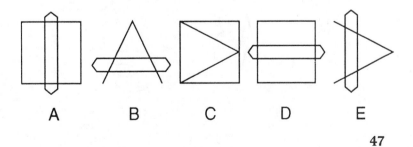

85. Your chemistry teacher asks you to convert temperatures from one system of measurement to another. These are new systems for determining temperatures, so, the classic conversions from Centigrade, Fahrenheit, and Kelvin don't apply.

You are told that 14° in the first system is equal to 36° in the second system. You also know that 133° in the first system is equal to 87° in the second.

What is the method or formula for converting one system to the other?

At what temperature will both thermometers read the same?

86. One of these figures doesn't belong with the rest. Don't be concerned about symmetry. Which doesn't belong? Why?

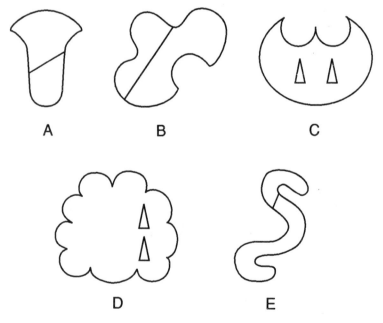

A   B   C

D   E

87. How many different squares of any size are in this figure?

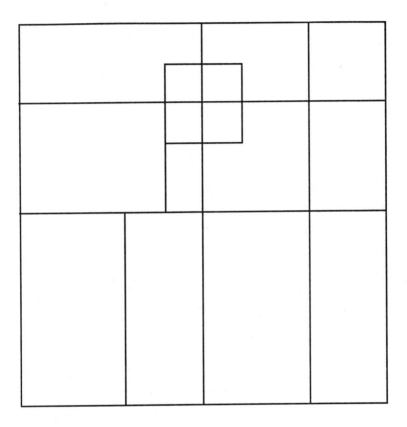

88. Apollona Constantino has 57 of them. Maggie Lieber has 36 of them. Paul Furstenburg has 45 of them. Based on the above, how many of them does Mary Les have?

89. How many individual cubes are in this configuration? All rows and columns in the figure are complete unless you actually see them end.

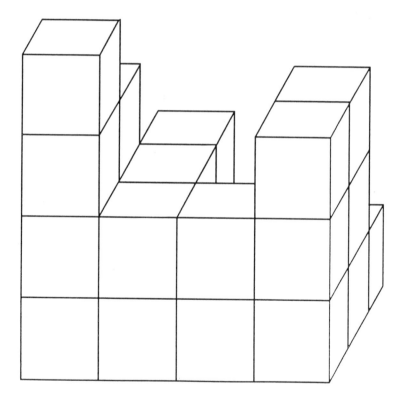

90. Thirteen boys and girls wait to take their seats in the same row in a movie theater. The row is thirteen seats long. They decide that after the first person sits down, the next person has to sit next to the first. The third sits next to one of the first two and so on until all thirteen are seated. In other words, no person can take a seat that separates him from at least one other person.

How many different ways can this be accomplished, assuming that the first person can choose any of the thirteen seats?

ANSWERS

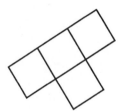
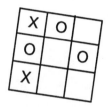

1. Construct a chart to consider the possible values.

E	1	2	3	4	5	6	7	8	9
CARRYOVERS N	4	8	1 2	1 6	2 0	2 4	2 8	3 2	3 6
4N + CARRYOVERS	6	2	9	5	2	8	4	1	7

E cannot equal zero since that would make N zero. We need a value where four E's equal N and four N's are equal to E plus a carryover. From the chart, we see that the only place where that occurs is when E equals 2. Therefore, E = 2, N = 8, and O must equal 1, since any number greater than that would result in an additional carryover.

$$\begin{array}{r} 182 \\ 182 \\ 182 \\ \underline{182} \\ 728 \end{array}$$

2. When referring to columns, they are numbered from left to right. In the first column, N + M + S is equal to a number less than 10. Therefore, the greatest number of the three could be a 6 with no carryover from the second column, or a 5 with a carryover from the second column. Obviously, there is a carryover from, or to, at least one of the two middle columns, since their sums yield two different letters.

Let's make an assumption that there is a carryover to the first column, and, therefore, no number can be greater than 5 in that column.

Now consider the possibilities for the last column.

N	1	2	3	4	5
CARRYOVERS				1	1
E	3	6	9	2	5

N cannot equal 5, because then E would equal 5. If N = 1, O would have to be 7, which is impossible, since the sum of the second column would then be 23. N cannot equal 3 because there are no digits which when multiplied by 3 have 3 as a result. N cannot equal 4 because that would mean that O would equal 1, and both remaining numbers in the first column would be greater than 4. Therefore, N equals 2 and E equals 6.

If N is 2, then O must be 4. Since we have the numbers 2, 3, and 4 accounted for, M + S can only equal 1 and 5, and they are interchangeable.

```
 2442
 5442
 1442
 ────
 9326
```

3. Here are two solutions. Can you find others?

```
      8026              8096
        26                96
       938               748
      1280              1980
      ────              ────
    10,270            10,920
```

4. Since it is known that A + B = Z, it then follows that A + B + P = T. We also know that T + A = F, so in the equation B + P + F = 24, we can replace F with T + A. The equation then becomes B + P + T + A = 24 or B + P + T = 22, since A = 2. Then we have:

$$
\begin{array}{r}
+\ B + P + 2 = T \\
-\ B - P + 22 = T \\
\hline
24 = 2T
\end{array}
$$

So, T = 12. Now, 12 + A = 14 = F, and Q − 12 = 17. So, Q = 19, and, therefore, S = 5.

5. View C is not correct.

6. Besides the one shown in Puzzle 5 and the two in this puzzle, eight other ways are possible.

7. It is always helpful to set up a legend of what is given and to work from there.

$$X = \$ .50 \text{ pens}$$
$$Y = \$5.50 \text{ pens}$$
$$Z = \$9.50 \text{ pens}$$

Set up two equations as follows:

$$X + Y + Z = 100$$

$$\$.50X = \$5.50Y + \$9.50Z = 100$$

Now, we need at least one of the values to drop out in order to consider the other two. Multiply the first equation by $-.5$ to drop X out of both equations.

$$
\begin{array}{rrrr}
-0.5X & -0.5Y & -0.5Z = & -50 \\
+0.5X & +5.5Y & +9.5Z = & 100 \\
\hline
& +5.0Y & +9.0Z = & 50
\end{array}
$$

$$5Y = 50 - 9Z$$
$$Y = 10 - \tfrac{9}{5}Z$$

Since we're dealing with whole numbers, Z must be a whole number and a multiple of 5. In this case, Z can only equal 5. With any greater number, Y will become a negative number. So, $Z = 5$ and Y becomes 1, leaving X to be 94 pens at \$.50.

$$94 \text{ pens at } \$ .50$$
$$1 \text{ pen } \text{ at } \$5.50$$
$$5 \text{ pens at } \$9.50$$

8. B, C, and D form the triangle.

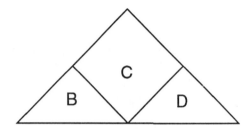

9. Q, K, Q, Q, K, K, and K is the order that works.

10.

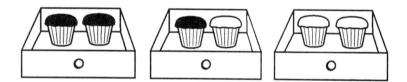

As you can see, there are only three possibilities where a chocolate cupcake could be chosen first.

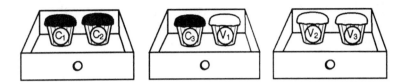

Out of these three, there are only two where a chocolate cupcake could be chosen second.

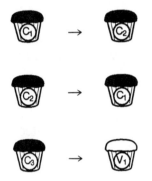

The answer is two out of three.

11. If the first digit of the four-digit code cannot be 0, 5, or 7, that leaves seven possible numbers for the first digit. All ten digits, however, can be used for the second, third, and fourth numbers.

$$7 \times 10 \times 10 \times 10$$

There are 7,000 possible different code words.

12. Columns are numbered from left to right. There has to be a carryover of 2 to the first column. If P were 9 and Q were 8, with a carryover of 1 from the last column, the sum of 20 could not be reached if R equaled 1. Therefore, R cannot be 1.

13. The powers of 7 have a repeating pattern for the last digit that can be found easily without performing the entire multiplication of each power.

7^0	7^1	7^2	7^3	7^4	7^5	7^6	7^7
1	7	9	3	1	7	9	3

With a repeating pattern of four, 7^{32} has the same remainder as 7^0, which is 1. Then 7^{33} would be in the next column, 7^1. Its remainder is 7 when divided by 10.

14. Normally, newspapers are printed on one large sheet. In a finished section, the first and second pages are printed on half of the sheet, and the second to last and last page are on the front and back of the other half. Therefore, the final page of a section of newspaper is usually a multiple of 4. In this case, pages 1 and 2 are attached to 39 and 40 (since the section contains 40 pages). The rest of the pages are attached like this.

1–2	39–40
3–4	37–38
5–6	35–36
7–8	33–34
9–10	31–32
11–12	29–30
13–(14)	(27–28)
15–16	25–26
17–18	23–24
19–20	21–22

The three missing pages are 14, 27, and 28.

15. This type of puzzle is a form of syllogism. It can best be shown by using Venn diagrams.

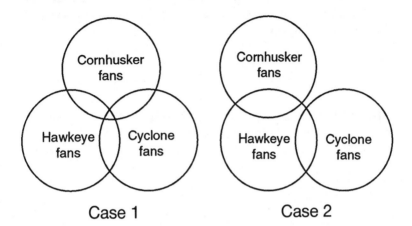

Case 1   Case 2

From Case 1, we can see that it is possible for a Cornhusker to be a Cyclone fan, but from Case 2, it is not definite. The conclusion is false.

16. Obviously, their number system is based on something other than 10. Let's say it is based on a notation represented by N.

$3N + 0$, their number 30, is the number we call 24.

You can reason that $3N + 0 = 24$, and $N = 8$.

Likewise, $3N + 4 = 28$, and $N = 8$.

Their number system is then $BASE_8$ and $5 \times 4 \times 7$, our 140, becomes their 214.

8^2	8^1	8^0
2	1	4

17. Since Dave spoke to the biologist, and Ann was sitting next to the chemist and across from the doctor, Cathy must be the author, and Ann is the biologist. The doctor didn't speak, but Dave did. So, Bobbie is the doctor and Dave is the chemist.

18. With two players for each match through seven rounds, 2^7 or 128 players enter.

19. Turn the first grid 90° to the right, and delete the bottom row of figures. Then turn the result 90° to the right again and delete the bottom row. Do the same with the third grid to get the answer.

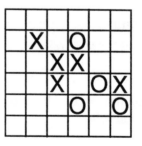

20. The sum is ⅓. Can you determine what the sum is of the infinite series ⅓ + ⅑ + ¹⁄₂₇ + ¹⁄₈₁ . . .?

21. You can approach this puzzle in several ways.

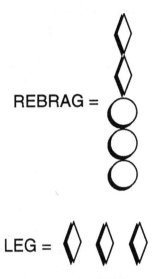

REBRAG =

LEG =

One of the first things you may have noticed is that the horizontal figures both contain an L, whereas the two vertical figures contain an R. The equations with two figures both contain a B and the equations with three figures both have a G. The circles have an A and the diamonds an E for their lone vowels. So, that yields this basic information.

$$L = \text{horizontal} \qquad B = 2$$
$$R = \text{vertical} \qquad A = \bigcirc$$
$$G = 3 \qquad E = \Diamond$$

22. In the first two foreign phrases, *roi* is the only common word. The word "three" in the English version is likewise the only common word; so, *roi* means "three." In the second and third foreign phrases, the word *kir* is used. The English translations share the word meaning "coins." So, *kir* means coins. Comparing the first and third phrases, we see they share the word *kaf*, meaning "take." Therefore, *kaf* means "take." From the English translation of the first phrase, *"Kaf navcki roi,"* we know that *navcki* means "pieces." From the second phrase, *palt* must mean "hide," and from the third phrase, *inoti* means "cautiously."

"Hide pieces cautiously" becomes *"Palt navcki inoti,"* assuming that the foreign syntax follows that of English.

23. From left to right in the diagram, the weights are 4, 6, and 30 pounds. From the hint, we know that the weight times the distance on the left side of the mobile (left and right are separated by the supporting wire from the ceiling) must equal the weight times the distance on the right side.

The diagram shows that the 4-foot segment in the middle of the mobile supports 5 pounds. Thus, 4 feet × 5 pounds = 20 foot pounds that must be equalled on the left side of the same segment. Since the left side of this segment is 2 feet long, it must support 10 pounds (2 feet × 10 pounds = 4 feet × 5 pounds). The total of the first two question marks is 10 pounds. That 10 pounds must be split in a 3 to 2 ratio, since one segment is 3 feet long, and the other is 2 feet long. Four pounds will be under the 3-foot segment, and 6 pounds will be under the 2-foot segment (3 feet × 4 pounds + 2 feet × 6 pounds).

There are a total of 75 pounds on the left side, supported by a 2-foot segment that is connected to the wire from the ceiling. Thus, for the left side, 2 feet × 75 pounds = 150 foot pounds. On the right side, we need a weight times the 5-foot length that will produce 150 foot pounds, or 5 feet × weight = 150 foot pounds. So, the weight is 30 pounds on the right side.

Or, if you worked this out in metrics, the weights are 1.8 kilograms, 2.7 kilograms, and 13 kilograms, from right to left on the diagram.

24. The probability is 14.3 percent. Twenty-two percent of the people are not gum chewers and 65 percent are over fifteen years old. Therefore, 22 percent × 65 percent or 14.3 percent are not gum chewers and are above the age of fifteen.

25. The only relationship these capital letters have is that their shapes are totally or partially closed. R is the next and last letter of the alphabet that meets this requirement.

26. The answer is E. A is larger than B by 1. This is a good example of reducing a seemingly difficult problem to an example that is workable.

For instance, $2^5 = 32$.

$$2^4(16) + 2^3(8) + 2^2(4) + 2^1(2) + 2^0(1) = 31$$

That is 1 less than 32.

27. It only took John four steps to accomplish his task.

Step 1—John filled the five-gallon bucket and poured all of it into the six-gallon bucket.

Step 2—He refilled the five-gallon bucket and poured out one gallon into the six-gallon bucket to fill it, leaving four gallons in the five-gallon bucket.

Step 3—He dumped the six-gallon bucket and poured the four gallons from the five-gallon bucket into the six-gallon bucket.

Step 4—Then, John refilled the five-gallon bucket and started home for a piece of cake.

28. EMIT spelled backwards is TIME. STAR spelled backwards is RATS.

29. The next number is 4. Here's how to set up the problem.

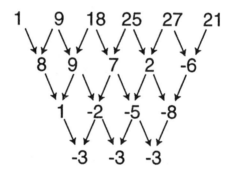

If the difference of the numbers of the series is taken to the end, a pattern of − 3 is established. The next number in the series must yield a − 3 in the bottom row. The number next to − 8 must be − 11. Next to − 6 is a − 17, and 4 is next to 21.

So, here's how we complete the diagram of the setup.

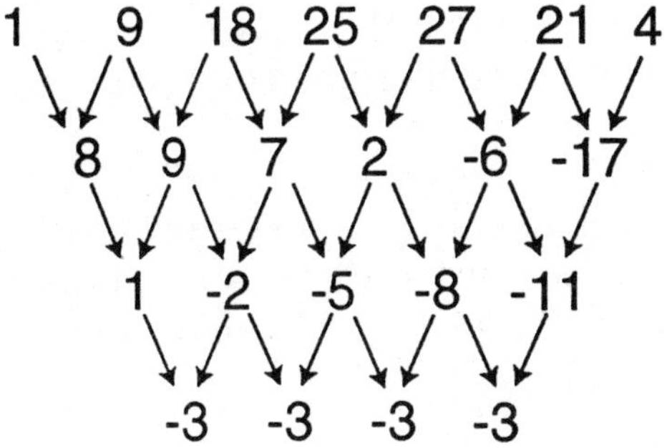

1   9   18   25   27   21   4

8   9   7   2   -6   -17

1   -2   -5   -8   -11

-3   -3   -3   -3

30. In one day, nine men work at a rate of X compared to seven women who work at a rate of Y. This can be expressed as:

$$9X + 7Y = \tfrac{1}{5}$$

Likewise in the second case:

$$7X + 11Y = \tfrac{1}{4}$$

Taking these two equations together, we have:

$$9X + 7Y = \tfrac{1}{5}$$
$$7X + 11Y = \tfrac{1}{4}$$

$$45X + 35Y = 1$$
$$28X + 44Y = 1$$

$$45X + 35Y = 28X + 44Y$$
$$17X = 9Y$$

$$\frac{Y \text{ or women's rate}}{X \text{ or men's rate}} = \frac{17}{9}$$

The women are better workers by a ratio of 17 to 9.

31. The answer is 6119. These are four consecutive numbers that read the same right side up as they do upside down.

32. The next number is 224. Notice that no digit is greater than 4. That's because these are the $BASE_{10}$ numbers 1, 2, 4, 8, 16, 32, and 64 converted to numbers in $BASE_5$.

33. The missing number is 1. This is the fraction $\frac{1}{7}$ converted to decimal form.

34. The number is 8. Starting with the first and last numbers and working towards the middle, each pair of numbers totals 20.

35. The next number is 30. This is actually two different series contained within one. One series begins with 0 and continues with every other number. Likewise, starting with the 2, a second series is established with every other number.

36. The missing number is 5. Each number stands for a letter of the alphabet where A = 1, B = 2, C = 3, etc. The word spelled out is *PUZZLES*.

37. The answer is 51. In this problem, the differences between the numbers forms a pattern, allowing you to predict the next numbers. After finding the difference, find the difference of the resulting numbers.

38. The correct number is 51. These numbers represent the answers for each of the six problems starting with Puzzle 32.

39. Unscrambled, the letters spell out *ALBERT EINSTEIN*.

40. The maximum number of cubes is nineteen.

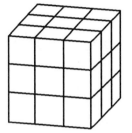

41. There are several different methods of approaching this problem. Since there are three unknowns, it is helpful to establish whatever relationship may exist between the unknowns and then attempt to express that relationship in common terms.

Looking at the first two parts of the equations, we see that § = 2⊗.

We know that ¶ − § = 6 and, therefore, § = ¶ − 6, which means that 2⊗ = ¶ − 6.

If we replace each § with 2⊗, we then have 7⊗ = 2¶.

Solving for ⊗ in the third equation, we have ⊗ = $\frac{¶ - 6}{2}$.

Solving for ⊗ in the fourth equation, we have ⊗ = $\frac{2¶}{7}$.

$$\frac{¶ - 6}{2} = \frac{2¶}{7} \qquad 3¶ = 42$$

$$7(¶ - 6) = 4¶ \qquad ¶ = 14$$

$$7¶ - 42 = 4¶ \qquad \begin{array}{l} § = 8 \\ ⊗ = 4 \end{array}$$

42. From several thousand feet high, the pyramid would look like this:

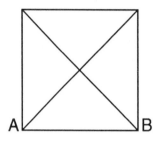

The 60° angle between Lines A and B would appear to be 90° to Judy.

43. Each X moves clockwise on the outside squares. Each O moves counterclockwise.

X	O	
O		O
X		

44. Think of the two figures as an opaque rectangle that has an opaque square behind it. To arrive at the second part of the analogy, the square (the bottom figure) rotates 45° in either direction, and the rectangle (the top figure) rotates 90° in either direction.

To find the correct solution, rotate the rectangle (now the bottom figure) 45°, and rotate the square (now the top figure) 90°. The answer is C.

45. Consider the first figure in the analogy to be two transparent triangles sharing a common base. Let the triangle on the left flip downwards, using the base as an axis. This will give you the second figure. Likewise, in the third figure, let the line connected to the circle on the left fall around the base. C is the answer.

46. A cube is made up of six planes; a tetrahedron has four planes. A triangle has three planes, so it needs two lines to keep it in the same 6 to 4 (3 to 2) ratio. Only A works.

47. In the first two figures of the analogy, place the vertical line of the second figure directly behind the vertical line of the first. Where two flags meet on the same side of line, they turn into a square on the third figure. Where a flag and a circle meet, they cancel each other out, and no figure appears. If flags or circles are unopposed, they appear as they are on their respective sides of the combined lines. The result is:

48. C is the only figure that can't be completed with one continuous line that does not retrace any part of the figure.

49. Think it's impossible? It can be done.

The northbound train pulls into the siding, leaving its tail end hanging out on the main track. Meanwhile, the southbound train stays beyond the north switch of the siding, on the main track. When the northbound train stops just short of Point Z (in railroad terms, "in the clear of the main track"), the crew signals the southbound train to proceed south on the main track.

After the southbound train has pulled down fifty or sixty cars, it stops. At Point Z, one of its crew members makes a cut on the fifty or so cars of the southbound train. The southbound train pulls far enough down the main track to allow the northbound train to get out of the siding. The southbound train will have enough room to pull down and not interfere with the cars from the northbound train that are still on the main track.

The crew from the northbound train lines the switch at the top end of the siding, and the northbound train proceeds north, coupling its engine onto the remaining cars of the southbound train. It shoves north, leaving the siding completely. A member of the southbound train's crew lines the bottom end of the siding switch for the main track, and the southbound train pulls its car down two miles or so and stops. Another crew member lines the switch at the top end of the siding for the main track.

The northbound train proceeds south. The engine is pushing its 100 cars and pulling the remaining cars from the southbound train. When the northbound train (now travelling south) gets all its cars past the bottom or southern end of the siding, it lines the siding switch and shoves the remaining cars from the southbound train into the siding. When it comes back out, a crew member lines the switch for the main track, and the train proceeds north with its entire train intact.

The southbound train shoves back to the siding, picks up its remaining cars, and heads south with its entire train. (Hopefully, the crew of the southbound train will line the bottom siding switch for the main track after they pull out, so the next train won't have an open siding switch to worry about.)

50. Since Gear R has to make a complete trip around both fixed gears, it doesn't make any difference where we begin. For clarity's sake, we'll start as shown here.

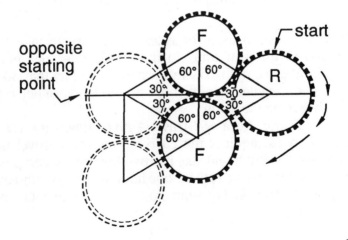

Keep in mind that if Gear R were to revolve around only the top fixed gear, it would make two revolutions, since their diameters are the same. Therefore, Gear R will make one revolution when it reaches the position of the dashed circle.

In order for Gear R to continue to a position opposite its starting point, it needs to travel 60° more, as shown. Since 60°/180° = ⅓, Gear R makes an additional ⅓ revolution, for a total of 1⅓ revolutions to its halfway point. Multiply that by 2 for the whole rotation, and you find that the answer is 2⅔ revolutions.

51. In a twelve-hour period starting after either 6 A.M. or 6 P.M., there will be eleven times when the hands are directly opposite each other. Twelve hours divided by eleven equals 1 hour, 5 minutes, and 27³/₁₁ seconds. Go back the 1 hour, 5 minutes, and 27³/₁₁ seconds from 6 o'clock, and you get 4:54 and 32⁸/₁₁ seconds.

52. Rendrag paid $120 for the entire trip, so for the half of the trip the students were travelling, Rendrag paid $60.00. For the price to be mathematically equitable, the students would each pay $20 to Rendrag for a total of $40. Rendrag's portion for this part of the trip is $20 also.

53. The question asks for rates. These are usually expressed in units of time, in this case, miles per hour (m.p.h.). We are not really interested in the fact that Sara may have travelled two or more hours, because her rate will always be the same.

In one hour, Sara will travel 4 miles down the river. Coming back, against the current, she must travel the same 4 miles, but it will take her two hours to accomplish this. In order to get a rate for one hour, we have to find out how far she travelled against the current in one hour, and that is 2 miles.

Sara travels a total of 6 miles in two hours for a rate of 3 m.p.h. Since she has gone up and down the river, the rate of the river is cancelled out, and Sara's rate is 3 m.p.h. (6 miles divided by two hours) in still water, which means the rate of the river is 1 m.p.h.

54. The missing letter is R. The letters spell out "What is the answer?"

55. The sum of the three numbers below the diameter equals ⅓ of the top number. So, the answer is one.

56. Candace is Jane's niece.

57. Ten weights will balance either 50 gold coins or 40 silver coins. Since only 20 gold coins are used, that means the weight of 30 gold coins is to be used by the silver coins. The weights are in a 4-to-5 ratio, and ⅘ of 30 = 24. So, 24 silver coins should be added to the 20 gold coins to balance the 10 weights.

58. Here are the answers.

$$A = 3$$
$$B = 1$$
$$C = 4$$
$$D = 2$$

59. The 2-inch hose will drain the water faster, since it has a bigger spout area than the two 1-inch hoses. The area of a circle is given by multiplying π (3.14) times the radius squared. The radius of the 2-inch hose is 1 inch. Its area is equal to $\pi \times 1 \times 1$ or π square inches. The area of the two 1-inch hoses is:

$$\pi \times \tfrac{1}{2} \times \tfrac{1}{2} + \pi \times \tfrac{1}{2} \times \tfrac{1}{2}$$

or $\dfrac{\pi}{4} + \dfrac{\pi}{4}$, which equals $\dfrac{\pi}{2}$ square inches

The 2-inch hose drains water twice as fast.

60. The 8 and 7 are interchangeable.

6	2184
+ 6	2970
12	5154

61.

41067
41607
$826743

62. The numbers are the numbers on the telephone, as shown here.

ABC	DEF	GHI	JKL	MNO	PRS	TUV	WXY
2	3	4	5	6	7	8	9

If the number is slanted to the left, then the left-most letter of that grouping is the letter to be used. If it is slanted to the right, the right-most letter is the choice. Letters that are straight up and down are represented by the center letter.

The note says, "Went to buy a new phone."

63. If 81 students had taken a course in geography, then only 9 students out of the 90 (10 took neither) took only geology. Since 63 students out of 90 had taken geology, that leaves 27 who had taken only geography.

$$27 + 9 = 36 \qquad \text{$^{36}/_{100}$ is 36 percent or $^{9}/_{25}$}$$

The answer is 36 percent or nine out of twenty-five.

Since 36 students took either geography or geology and 10 took neither, that leaves 54 percent who took at least one class in both.

64. Although the chances are remote, you just might pull the 24 blue socks out first. You'd need two more to make certain to get two black socks. You'd be assured of a pair of black socks by pulling 26 socks.

65. The two winning first moves are these.

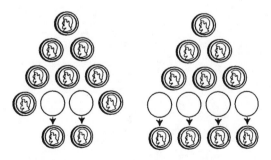

66. Let's work this out.

Obviously, 10 must be in the top row, but it cannot be in either of the first two positions, since that would result in a duplication of 5's. Since 7 can only result from either $8 - 1$ or $9 - 2$, 8 and 9 must be in the top or next row. Nine can only result from $10 - 1$, or it has to be in the top row. Therefore, 8 and 9 are not in the same row, and neither are 1 and 2, but all four numbers are in the top two rows. Out of the seven positions in the top two rows, we have 10, 9, 8, 1, 2, and 5 with 7 in the third row. That leaves 6, 3, or 4 for the remaining position in the top row. The digit next to the 7 can't be a 6 because that would result in duplicate 1's, and 6 cannot be the result of 7 minus any other number. Therefore, 6 is the remaining number of the seven numbers in the top two rows.

Six cannot be next to 5 or above 7; so, it must be in the top row with 10. But 6 cannot be next to 10; so, it is in the first or second position of the top row. And the number next to it must be 1. That means 9 cannot be in the top row; it would have to be next to 10, which would result in double 1's when subtracted. Eight must then be the other number in the top row.

That means the top row is 6   1   10   8, from which the remaining numbers can be generated:

$$6 \quad 1 \quad 10 \quad 8$$
$$5 \quad 9 \quad 2$$
$$4 \quad 7$$
$$3$$

For numbers 1 through 15:

$$13 \ 3 \ 15 \ 14 \ 6$$
$$10 \ 12 \ 1 \ 8$$
$$2 \ 11 \ 7$$
$$9 \ 4$$
$$5$$

67. The first two digits enclosed within any parentheses are added together to get the second number contained within each parentheses. To get the first two digits of any following parentheses, add the numbers found in the preceding parentheses together. In this case, that is:

$$37 : 10$$

68. Here's one way the letter cross could look.

4265
8
3
1790

The total of the numbers used is 51 (17 × 3). The total of the numbers 1 through 9 is 45. There is a difference of 6. That difference is found in the letters D and G, since they are the only two letters counted twice. D and G must equal 6, and E + F must equal 11 to total 17 in the column. Since A = 4, D and G must be 1 and 5. The number 7 cannot be E or F. It would require the 4 to total 11. Also, 7 cannot be B, C, or D, since 4 + 7 would require the remaining two numbers in the top row to total 6, which is impossible. Therefore, 7 is in the bottom row with 0. That means the bottom row needs two numbers (besides 7 and 0) to total 10 for G + H + I + J to equal 17. One of those numbers must be 1 or 5. It can't be 5. You'd then have two 5's to total 10. Therefore, D = 5, G = 1, and the remaining number in the bottom row is 9. At this point the puzzle looks like this.

$$4BC5$$
$$E$$
$$F$$
$$1790$$

E + F must equal 11. The possible combinations are these.

$$2 + 9$$
$$3 + 8$$
$$4 + 7$$
$$5 + 6$$

The only possibility out of this group is 3 + 8, solving the values for D, E, F, and G, leaving 6 and 2 for B and C.

69. The next one is 46656.

Disregarding the number 1, these are the four consecutive lowest numbers that are both cubes and squares.

64	**729**	**4096**
8^2 or 4^3	27^2 or 9^3	64^2 or 16^3

15625	and the fifth,	**46656**
125^2 or 25^3		216^2 or 36^3

70. Here's how to find the answer.

Since we know that Box C isn't the smallest, out of Boxes A, B, C, and D, Box D is the smallest. Its number is either 4 or 5.

The possible numbers for Box C are 2, 3, or 4 (not the largest or the smallest).

Box A can only be 2 or 3, since it is bigger than Box C or Box D, but it is not the biggest.

The total of Box C plus Box D must be at least 6 but not more than 7. The greatest sum of four different numbers between 1 and 5 is 7, assuming two different numbers equal two other different numbers.

Since Box A is 2 or 3, and its number plus Box E's number must be at least 6, Box E is either 4 or 5.

$$Box\ A\ =\ 2\ or\ 3$$
$$Box\ C\ =\ 2\ or\ 3$$
$$Box\ D\ =\ 4\ or\ 5$$
$$Box\ E\ =\ 4\ or\ 5$$

We know that Box A is bigger than Box C, so Box A = 2, Box C = 3, Box D = 4, Box E = 5, and Box B = 1.

71. Three out of eight chances. Here are the possibilities.

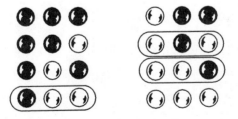

So, there are only three chances out of the eight possible combinations you could make.

83

72. Let's take a look at how this might be accomplished. Each letter represents a different person present at the gathering. Remember that when one person shakes another's hand, each person gets credit for a handshake. There are several ways to accomplish this. Here's one.

> X shakes hands with W, Y, Z, T.
> Y shakes hands with W, Z, T, X.
> W shakes hands with Z, T, X, Y.
> Z shakes hands with R, X, Y, W.
> T shakes hands with S, X, Y, W.

As can be seen from our chart, X, Y, W, Z, and T each have four handshakes. R and S each have one. So the minimum number of people needed to accomplish the required handshakes is seven. X, Y, W, Z, and T each have four handshakes, and R and S have one apiece for a total of twenty-two handshakes.

73. Below is a table showing different combinations and probabilities of the dice. From the total combinations, we can see that there are a total of thirty-six chances.

Total Number Showing on Dice	Total Combinations	Chances
2	1	$\frac{1}{36}$
3	2	$\frac{2}{36}$
4	3	$\frac{3}{36}$
5	4	$\frac{4}{36}$
6	5	$\frac{5}{36}$
7	6	$\frac{6}{36}$
8	5	$\frac{5}{36}$
9	4	$\frac{4}{36}$
10	3	$\frac{3}{36}$
11	2	$\frac{2}{36}$
12	1	$\frac{1}{36}$

You can see there are three ways to roll a 10 and six ways to roll a 7. Out of these nine possibilities, three are favorable for a win. Therefore, the chances for winning with 10 as a point are one in three.

74. Here are the remaining moves.

> 7—Move 1 to 4.
> 8—Move 15 to 6.
> 9—Move 6 to 13.
> 10—Move 12 to 14.
> 11—Move 4 to 13.
> 12—Move 14 to 12.
> 13—Move 11 to 13.

75. Believe it or not, fifteen pieces (maximum) will result with four straight cuts through a cube.

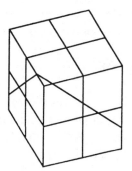

This formula will give you the answer for any number of cuts. N = the number of cuts. So, three planar cuts yields eight pieces, four planar cuts yields fifteen pieces, five planar cuts yields twenty-six pieces, and six planar cuts yields forty-two pieces, and so on.

$$\left(\frac{N^3 + 5N}{6} \right) + 1 = \text{Number of Pieces}$$

76. Let's see how its done. You only need to move five coins to turn the triangle upside down.

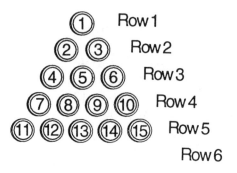

1—Move ③ to Row 3, outside ⑥.
2—Move ② to Row 3, outside ④.
3—Move ① to Row 6, between ⑫ and ⑬.
4—Move ⑮ to Row 6, between ⑬ and ⑭.
5—Move ⑪ to be the lone coin on the point of the upside-down triangle.

In general, where N is equal to the length of any side of a triangle (length in number of coins), the minimum number of coins that need to be moved to turn that triangle upside down can be found by this formula.

$$\frac{N(N+1)}{6}.$$

If the result of the division has a remainder, the answer is simply rounded down to the nearest whole number found in the quotient.

For example, if $N = 7$, then $\frac{7 \times 8}{6} = 6\overline{)56} = 9\frac{1}{3}$.

Rounding down to 9 will give the minimum number of coins needed to be moved in a triangle that has seven coins on a side.

Special thanks to mathematician Frank Bernhart (Rochester, N.Y.) for his assistance.

77. This object requires six cubes to build. Here is its orthographic projection.

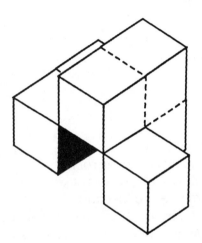

78. Here are the answers.

    A. far be it from me
    B. border patrol
    C. "Unfinished Symphony"
    D. a man among men
    E. shrinking violets
    F. "dashing through the snow"
    G. the lesser of two evils
    H. good with numbers

79. Regardless of which face of Cube 1 you start with, the tunnel cannot exit through Cubes 3, 5, or 8.

80. Here's how you figure it out.

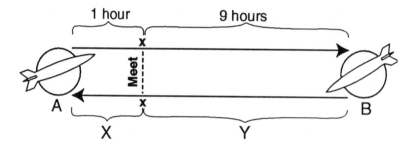

$$X + Y = \text{total distance}$$
V_f = velocity of faster rocket
V_s = velocity of slower rocket
T_b = time before meeting
Y = velocity of the faster rocket multiplied by the time before they meet ($V_f \times T_b$)
X = velocity of the slower rocket multiplied by the time before they meet ($V_s \times T_b$)

$$\text{Therefore, } \frac{X}{Y} = \frac{V_s}{V_f}$$

Now after the rockets meet, Y is equal to the slower velocity multiplied by 9, and X is equal to the faster velocity multiplied by one.

Thus:

$$\frac{X}{Y} = \frac{V_f}{9V_s}$$

We now have two different fractions that represent $\frac{X}{Y}$, and they are equal.

$$\frac{V_s}{V_f} = \frac{V_f}{9V_s}$$

$$V_f^2 = 9V_s^2$$

$$\sqrt{V_f^2} = \sqrt{9V_s^2}$$

$$V_f = 3V_s$$

The faster rocket is going three times as fast as the slower rocket.

81. If you are not careful, this short logic puzzle can be very confusing. Often, a solver's first instinct is to compare the speed and strength of each of the friends to determine their nicknames. Further inspection reveals that there isn't enough information to solve the puzzle that way. Here's where a grid of possibilities comes in handy.

We'll use X's and O's to fill in the grids. O will represent an elimination, and X will be a definite selection.

From a, we know that Pat can't be either the Rabbit or the Fly. So he must be either Bear or Walleye. We know from b that Tom cannot be either the Rabbit or Walleye. So he must be either Bear or Fly. So, let's begin to fill in the chart.

	Rabbit	Fly	Walleye	Bear
Bob				
Bill				
Pat	O	O		
Tom	O		O	

From c, we know that Bob can't be Bear or Rabbit. Since he is faster than both Pat and Bear, Pat must be Walleye (since Pat was either Walleye or Bear).

As you can see from the final chart, Bill must be Rabbit, Tom has to be Bear, and Bob must be Fly.

	Rabbit	Fly	Walleye	Bear
Bob	O	X	O	O
Bill	X	O	O	O
Pat	O	O	X	O
Tom	O	O	O	X

82. Here's one way.

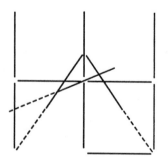

83. We know that Brand A and Brand B equal 40 pounds. We also know that 40 pounds times $7 a pound will equal $280. We can set up two equations that can be solved simultaneously.

$$A + B = 40 \text{ pounds}$$
$$9A + 4B = \$280$$

Multiply the first equation by − 9 to cancel out the A's.

$$
\begin{array}{r}
-9A - 9B = -360 \\
\underline{9A + 4B = 280} \\
-5B = -80
\end{array}
$$

B = 16 and, therefore, A = 24 pounds.

84. There are three different shapes to consider: a square, a loop, and two connecting lines. Figures A, B, and C each use two of the shapes. These first three figures form a pattern. Beginning with Figure D, the sequence continues. To get Figure D, Figure A was rotated 90° to the right. Figure E is really Figure B rotated 90° to the right. Therefore, the sixth figure will be Figure C rotated 90° to the right.

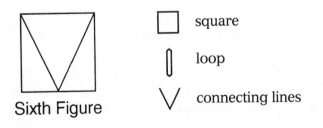

Sixth Figure

☐   square

◻ loop

∨   connecting lines

85. Let's call the first system X and the second system Y.

X	Y
14	36
133	87

In order to get an idea of some relationship between the two systems, we'll subtract 14 from 133 (119) and compare that to the difference of 87 minus 36 (51). We can compare 119 to 51, but first, let's reduce it by dividing by 17, giving us 7 to 3. For every seven degrees on the X thermometer, Y will grow or decrease by three. When X is at 14°, if we move toward X becoming 0°, Y will be reduced by 6°. When X is 0°, Y = 30°, giving us the formula Y = 3/7X + 30.

To find the temperature at which both thermometers read the same, set Y to equal X, and the formula then becomes:

$$X = \tfrac{3}{7}X + 30$$
$$\tfrac{4}{7}X = 30$$
$$4X = 210$$
$$X = 52.5°$$

86. The answer is D. The other four figures have both concave and convex components. Figure D has convex parts only.

87. There are fourteen squares.

88. The only thing you have to go on are the names of the people and the letters in their names. After a little inspection, you'll find each letter of the name is equivalent to three of "them," whatever "them" may be. Mary Les has seven letters in her name, therefore she has twenty-one of "them."

89. There are twenty-five individual cubes.

90. This a good example of a problem or puzzle that can be broken into smaller components to determine a pattern.

If one person walks into a theater to take one seat, that person has only one choice. If two people occupy two seats, this can happen in two different ways. Three people occupying three seats (following the condition that each subsequent person sits next to another) can be accomplished in four different ways. Four people in four seats produce eight ways. We'll make a table to see what we have.

Number of People	Possible Combinations
1	1
2	2
3	4
4	8
5	?

As can be seen, with each additional person and seat, the different orders increase by a power of two. For five people in five seats, there are sixteen different possible combinations. For any number N, it can be seen that $2^{(N-1)}$ will give the correct answer. So, for twelve people, 4096 different combinations are possible ($2^{(13-1)} = 2^{12} = 4096$).

INDEX

About the Author

Terry Stickels writes puzzle columns and creates brain-teasers for newspapers and magazines. He invented his first puzzle at age 11. He often appears as a guest speaker on critical thinking skills and puzzle topics for businesses and teachers, as well as for students in math and other junior and high school classes. He lives in Rochester, New York, and enjoys following college basketball and listening to rhythm-and-blues.